Praise for *I Am a Church Member*

There are scores of books on what it means to be a good pastor of a church. The same cannot be said for books on what it means to be a good member of a church. Thom Rainer helps cure the latter malady in this brief work that is biblical, simple and practical. This book is an easy read. It is also a convicting read. And, it is greatly needed when so many who attend church have a "what can I get" mentality rather than a "what can I give" mind-set. This book will serve the body of Christ well.

Daniel L. Akin
President, Southeastern Baptist Theological Seminary

I Am a Church Member is a resource that is long past due. It is simple, yet profound. We intend to use it at Sherwood in our Sherwood Story class and new member orientation. This book is a must read if you want your members to understand what it means to be committed to a local church. Read it and then buy copies for potential and new members. It will impact church health and help you close the back door.

Michael Catt
Senior Pastor, Sherwood Baptist Church
Executive Producer, Sherwood Pictures

One of the great privileges of my life is to pastor a local congregation of saints. Over the last decade I have seen first hand the fruits of those who understand the content of this book and don't just go to a church but belong to one. Dr. Rainer has served us all well in this book. He has wrung from the scriptures God's commands concerning the fullness of life found in Christ among his people in covenant faithfulness. If you love your church, are frustrated with your church, or don't understand why membership matters, I encourage you to pick this book up and read it.

Matt Chandler
Lead Pastor, Teaching, The Village Church

Church membership is the shape of Christian discipleship. Wise, simple and sweet, practical and even piercing—this brief volume, if read and digested, helps us to follow Christ. It comes complete with questions to be considered and pledges to be made. Thom Rainer has written a book to instruct new members and to remind long-time members that true discipleship may sometimes be heroic; it must always be humble.

Mark Dever
Senior Pastor, The Capitol Hill Baptist Church, Washington, DC
President, 9Marks

Thom Rainer, with this incredibly valuable little book, has once again demonstrated why he is considered a leader among church leaders. Though small in size, this insightful resource has the potential to bring about big results, helping to guide individuals and churches toward much-needed changes in how we all think about what is really involved in becoming a faithful church member. These thoughtful reflections, together with the illuminating and applicable responses, will serve as trustworthy steps toward health, renewal, and revitalization for congregations of all sizes.

David S. Dockery
President, Trinity International University

Timely. Needed. Powerful. Simple. Clear. Biblical. This book needs to be read by every pastor and church member globally. Find a way to get it to every Christ-follower. I will do all I can to do it in my church. Thank you for calling us back to the Bible!

Ronnie Floyd
Senior Pastor, Cross Church, Northwest Arkansas

For many years, the Lord has used Thom Rainer to encourage and challenge church leaders to be evangelistic, raise expectations, design a discipleship process, reach millennials, etc. And the church has benefited. Now, the Lord will use this helpful book to encourage church members to discover or rediscover the privilege and responsibility of belonging to a local church. And the church will benefit.

Eric Geiger
Senior Pastor, Mariners Church

Thom Rainer has tapped into a significant challenge in today's church that is experiencing a decline in church attendance and membership. *I Am a Church Member* focuses on the priority that all followers of Jesus Christ should emphasize and that is to serve Him by serving others based on the Biblical instruction set forth in Scripture. "Now [we] are the body of Christ and individual members of it" (1 Cor. 12:27). Thom has masterfully outlined how we should function within the context of the apostles' teaching and gives us pause to consider just how we should relate to others within the local church—Christ's words are to individuals that collectively make up the body of Christ. His work takes root in each individual heart.

Franklin Graham
President & CEO
Samaritan's Purse
Billy Graham Evangelistic Association

Thom paints the target right where it needs to be in his call to move the church from "consumer" to "disciple": our willingness (or lack thereof) to follow Jesus. This book is a timely, deeply challenging message for Western Christians. Combining the skill of a sociologist, the insight of a theologian and the wisdom of a practitioner, Thom has produced a book that easily qualifies for "best in class."

J.D. Greear
Lead Pastor, Summit Church, Raleigh-Durham, North Carolina
Author, *Stop Asking Jesus Into Your Heart: How To Know For Sure You Are Saved* and *Gospel: Recovering the Power That Made Christianity Revolutionary*

The church is the only bride of Christ. The church is the only plan of God to reach the world and it is the only organization that will last forever!

The Church (with a Big C) is only as strong as its local churches around the world. In a day of church decline and stagnation, it appears as if the church of today looks nothing like the church of the Bible.

I believe when ch... members around the world get a clear picture of what the Bible has to say about their relationship with their church—it will change the world! Thom Rainer has done it again. He has written a book that will advance the church and therefore advance the kingdom of God.

It is a must read for all church members everywhere.

Alex Himaya
Founding and Senior Pastor, TheChurch.at (BattleCreek/ Midtown), Tulsa, Oklahoma

As a church member I have the privilege to unite with the body of Christ in making an eternal difference through my giftedness in His service. Church membership is an honor, privilege, and joy. Where would I be without the fellowship, encouragement, and edifying of the church? I am so thankful to Thom Rainer for making that reality come alive in this book!

Johnny Hunt
Pastor, First Baptist Church of Woodstock, Georgia

Nothing compares to a group of believers who love one another, pray for each other, and serve God together to reach their neighbors and the nations. Few congregations meet this description, though. We have failed to teach about biblical church membership, and we have reaped what we've sown—membership without meaning and members without commitment. This little book will remind you and your church family that church membership carries both privilege AND responsibility. Had such a book been available years ago when I started pastoring, the churches I led would have been stronger churches. Indeed, I will be a better church member today after reading this book.

Chuck Lawless
Dean of Graduate Studies, Southeastern Seminary
Global Theological Education Consultant, International Mission Board

Think of this book as a church membership manifesto. Read it. Apply it. Get a copy of it for your pastor and every person on your leadership team. My friend, Thom Rainer, calls us to love the church and the members of it in a way that brings glory to God.

James MacDonald
Senior Pastor, Harvest Bible Chapel
Author, *Vertical Church*

Thom Rainer has created a profound and practical resource to help two generations of Christians—those who have become too comfortable and even apathetic in the church and those of my generation who are inclined to abandon it altogether. For those, like me, who have grown up in the church this is a pointed and necessary reminder of what it means to be a church member, and for those who are new to church it is a concise primer on the joy and life found in committing to a local church. I highly recommend this deep but uncomplicated book to any believer.

Barnabas Piper
Author and Podcaster

I always tell young business leaders that business is easy . . . until people get involved. Once you bring more than two people in, you're setting the stage for a lot of disagreements—and a lot of drama. The same is true for churches. In *I Am a Church Member*, Thom Rainer reminds us that it is possible to have an effective, unified church body—even if the people in the pews have different opinions.

Dave Ramsey
***New York Times* best-selling author and nationally syndicated radio show host**

What would happen if people didn't choose a church based on what they could receive from it but what they could give to it? What if they joined not only to be encouraged but to edify; not just to be served but to use their gifts and resources to serve? Dr. Rainer bravely and insightfully answers these questions in *I Am a Church Member*—a book that every single congregant needs to have in their hands. Small in size but mighty in impact, this resource will remind God's people of what the church was always intended to be and the power it was always meant to unleash. It is life giving and vision lending to a pastor and his people as they engage in community.

God's house, across the globe, will be better off because of it.

Priscilla Shirer
Bible Teacher and Author

According to Thom Rainer, Church membership doesn't simply have privileges; it is a privilege. And I couldn't agree more. In *I Am a Church Member* Thom delivers a biblical perspective and practical approach to church membership. This little book is both refreshing and inspirational. I couldn't put it down. I highly recommend you pick it up!

Andy Stanley
North Point Ministries

So much ink has been spilled to critique the church that it has almost become sport. Yet, I am confident that you cannot love Jesus and despise His wife, the Bride of Christ. Here, Thom Rainer offers a positive vision of healthy church membership and deep value for the bride of Christ. There's a deficit of books like the one in your hands, a rare treasure for a generation deeply in need of a compelling vision for this community called church.

Ed Stetzer
Billy Graham Distinguished Chair, Wheaton College

Simple, profound, practical and convicting. These are some of the words that came to mind after devouring *I Am a Church Member*. Thom Rainer shares what Christians need: basic building blocks for the body of believers.

Dave Stone
Senior Pastor, Southeast Christian Church, Louisville, Kentucky

I Am a Church Member is a great resource for both church leaders and church members. In a world obsessed with consumerism Dr. Rainer shows that, as a biblical church member, I am called to a greater commitment. I recommend that any church that takes belonging seriously consider giving a copy to every member.

Geoff Surratt
Managing Director, Exponential

Following Jesus involves far more than believing; it involves BELONGING. Only as we belong to Christ's Body can we become what He intends us to be. In fact, it is impossible to grow to spiritual maturity by yourself. You must be connected to the other parts of the Body. This wonderful little book explains the power of belonging to a church family.

Rick Warren
Pastor, Saddleback Church

Being a member of a local church is more than merely having a church to belong to. It's your way of committing to the work God is doing in us and through us as a community of believers. It's why you'll joyfully help to unify others versus gossiping about others. It's why you'll seek to serve sacrificially instead of being self-serving. Often, these principles don't come naturally which is why you need to read this book. *I Am a Church Member* will help you understand what membership is really all about and what a gift it is.

Pete Wilson
Senior Pastor, Cross Point Church, Nashville, Tennessee

Other Books by Thom S. Rainer

Scrappy Church
Becoming a Welcoming Church
We Want You Here
Who Moved My Pulpit?
I Will
Autopsy of a Deceased Church
The Millennials (coauthor)
Transformational Church (coauthor)
Simple Life (coauthor)
Essential Church (coauthor)
Vibrant Church (coauthor)
Raising Dad (coauthor)
Simple Church (coauthor)
The Unexpected Journey
Breakout Churches
The Unchurched Next Door
Surprising Insights from the Unchurched
Eating the Elephant (revised edition) (coauthor)
High Expectations
The Every Church Guide to Growth (coauthor)
The Bridger Generation
Effective Evangelistic Churches
The Church Growth Encyclopedia (coeditor)
Experiencing Personal Revival (coauthor)
Giant Awakenings
Biblical Standards for Evangelists (coauthor)
Eating the Elephant
The Book of Church Growth
Evangelism in the Twenty-first Century (editor)

I AM
A
CHURCH
MEMBER

Discovering
the Attitude
that Makes
the Difference

THOM S.
RAINER

B&H
PUBLISHING GROUP
NASHVILLE, TENNESSEE

978-1-4336-7973-5

Published by B&H Publishing Group
Nashville, Tennessee

Dewey Decimal Classification: 254.5
Subject Heading: CHURCH MEMBERSHIP \
CHURCH \ LAITY

All Scripture quotations are taken from the Holman Christian
Standard Bible (HCSB,) Copyright © 1999, 2000, 2002, 2003,
2009 by Holman Bible Publishers. Used by permission.

19 20 21 22 23 • 24 23 22 21 20

To

Brad Waggoner

Exemplary Leader
Devoted Churchman
Great Friend

∾

And always to

Nellie Jo

Devoted Wife
Best Friend
Joy Incarnate

Contents

Acknowledgments   xv

Introduction: A Tale of Two Church Members   1

CHAPTER 1   I Will Be a Functioning
             Church Member   9

CHAPTER 2   I Will Be a Unifying Church Member   21

CHAPTER 3   I Will Not Let My Church Be
             about My Preferences and Desires   33

CHAPTER 4   I Will Pray for My Church Leaders   43

CHAPTER 5   I Will Lead My Family to Be
             Healthy Church Members   55

CHAPTER 6   I Will Treasure Church
             Membership as a Gift   67

Acknowledgments

It may not take a village to write a book, but there is really no such thing as solo authorship. So many people are a part of this book, and most of those people are indispensable parts of my life.

I love my family. I really do love my family. I love my wife Nellie Jo. I love my sons Sam, Art, and Jess. I love my daughters-in-law Erin, Sarah, and Rachel. And I love my grandchildren Canon, Maggie, Nathaniel, Harper, and Bren. I love my grandson Will, who is in heaven, and I can't wait to see him again. I mention my family first because they are first in my life. I could not accomplish anything, like writing a book, without the love and encouragement of my family. Did I mention that I really do love my family?

My life is so much richer because God led me to LifeWay Christian Resources. I am a most blessed man to serve alongside thousands of the greatest servant employees anywhere in the world. God is truly working through these men and women. I express specific gratitude to my super editors and friends, Jedidiah Coppenger and Jennifer Lyell. And I am ever grateful for the incredible leadership of Selma Wilson over B&H Publishing Group. I don't claim perfection in my leadership at LifeWay, but I must say that asking Selma to lead B&H was one of the smartest leadership moves I have made. Thanks also to Amy Jordan, my executive assistant, better known as Superwoman. Amy can manage any situation because she can manage me.

This book is not only dedicated to my wife, Nellie Jo; it is also dedicated to Brad Waggoner. Brad is the executive vice president of LifeWay. Let me state it simply: I could not lead LifeWay without the leadership of Brad Waggoner. I am so dependent upon his strategic mind, his voice of wisdom, and his ability to get to the heart of any issue. And to make our relationship even richer, Brad is one of my best friends in the world.

Ultimately, though, I give this book to the glory of God. It is a book about Christ's Church. The Father so loved the world that He sent His Son to die for His Church. It is my prayer that this little tome will strengthen local congregations. And I pray that those who are members of these churches will see the incredible gift of belonging to the body of Christ.

Thank you for reading this book. Thank you for reading it prayerfully. And thank you for your willingness to be changed by the power of the Holy Spirit to be a more devoted and sacrificial member of the bride of Christ.

Introduction

A Tale of Two Church Members

Michael and Liam began meeting for Monday morning breakfast at six o'clock over five months ago. They originally thought it would be a one-time event. They met in a couples' Bible study group in their church. For many different reasons they hit it off and were becoming good friends. When Michael originally invited Liam to meet him for breakfast on a Monday morning several months ago, Liam readily agreed.

The two men enjoyed their time together so much that the one-time event became a weekly event. It was now rare for the two friends not to meet on Monday morning.

Early in their friendship the conversations focused on sports, family, and politics. They had much in common. Michael was forty-one and Liam was thirty-nine. They each had three kids, and they were both college football fanatics. Each of their teams was in the same football conference, but they were pretty fierce rivals as well. The guys thoroughly enjoyed trash-talking the other's team in a friendly spirit.

But on this particular Monday morning, the conversation turned serious. Michael and his wife had noticed some changes in the demeanor of Liam in their Bible study group. He no longer seemed as interested in studying and discussing the Bible as he did talking about their church. And his comments were often critical about the congregation where the two families both had their memberships.

Still, Michael was caught off guard on that particular Monday morning. Liam loved the poached eggs in the little restaurant; it was his regular order. But on this Monday morning, he had not touched them. He was barely sipping his coffee.

Liam didn't take long to get to the point. "Michael," he began, "Lana and I have decided to leave the church." The pause seemed to last minutes. Neither of the men seemed to know who should speak next. Michael took the initiative and spoke softly and deliberately.

"You want to tell me about it?" Michael inquired. He honestly didn't know if Liam wanted to say anymore about it. His friend seemed resolute. Nevertheless, Liam began to explain his feelings and decision.

"Lana and I went to the church to learn deep truths about the Bible," Liam offered. "But Pastor Robert is just not feeding us. We're not getting anything out of his messages. Sitting in the service on Sunday morning is just a waste of our time."

Michael didn't respond. He could tell Liam had more to say.

"There are several great people in the church," Liam continued. "You and Karen are the best, and there are a few more like you." He paused and his facial expression became even more serious. "But, honestly, Michael, our church is full of hypocrites. Did you hear Jim at the kids' basketball game? He embarrassed me the way he was screaming at the refs. What kind of testimony is that for a Christian? And of course, everyone knows about Neal. He was supposedly this pillar of the church, and we find out he's been cheating on his wife for over a year. What kind of church is this with these kinds of people?"

Liam was angry but controlled as he continued to vent. "Look, Pastor Robert acts like he cares for us, but I'm not so sure he does. I told him that Lana's dad was in the hospital for hernia surgery, and he never visited him."

Michael knew that Lana's father was not a church member, and he lived fifty miles away. He also knew that Pastor Robert called him and had prayer with him. But he also knew that any rebuttal would not be appreciated at the moment. Michael held his tongue.

Now it seemed that Liam's mild rant was winding down. Liam seemed exhausted, ready to bring the conversation to a close. He did, however, offer a few pointed comments and two insightful questions.

"Michael," Liam began softly. "I really like you and Karen and your kids. All of you are a class act." He paused briefly. "But you seem enthused about the church. You keep serving and contributing. Don't take me wrong, but I wonder at times if you are blind to all the problems in the church."

Then Liam offered a closing that really spoke more than he realized.

"We are really two different types of church members," he stated. "Why is that? Why do we have such different perspectives?"

The Difference

Based on our research of 557 churches from 2004 to 2010, nine out of ten churches in America are declining or growing at a pace that is slower than that of their communities. Simply stated, churches are losing ground in their own backyards.

Another way of looking at it is generationally. About two-thirds of the Builder generation, those born before 1946, are Christians. But only 15 percent of the Millennials are Christians. The Millennials are the largest generation in America's history with almost eighty million members. They were born between 1980 and 2000. And we have all but lost that generation.

We can blame it on the secular culture. And we often do.

We can blame it on the godless politics of our nation. We do that as well.

We can even blame it on the churches, the hypocritical members, and the uncaring pastors. Lots of Christians are doing that.

But I am proposing that we who are church members need to look in the mirror. I am suggesting that congregations across America are weak because many of us church members have lost the biblical understanding of what it means to be a part of the body of Christ.

We join our churches expecting others to serve us, to feed us, and to care for us.

We don't like the hypocrites in the church, but we fail to see our own hypocrisies.

God did not give us local churches to become country clubs where membership means we have privileges and perks.

He placed us in churches to serve, to care for others, to pray for leaders, to learn, to teach, to give, and, in some cases, to die for the sake of the gospel.

Many churches are weak because we have members who have turned the meaning of membership upside down. It's time to get it right. It's time to become a church member as God intended. It's time to give instead of being entitled.

The Journey

Join me on this journey of discovering or rediscovering the privilege and the joy of church membership. And before you get too caught up in the meaning of church membership, take time to read the next brief chapter. Let us then take six steps carefully and prayerfully. And at the end of each step, let us be willing to make a commitment, a real commitment to our church.

When this journey is over for you, two things will likely take place. First, you will likely have a new or renewed attitude about your church. You will learn the joy of being last instead of seeking to be first. Instead of being a whiner complaining about what's wrong with your church, you will be a unifier seeking what's best for your church.

Second, your church will begin to change. It will become healthier because one of its members is healthier. And as the church gets healthier, it will have a greater impact on its community and the world.

We may just discover that the reason our nation is in such bad shape is because our churches are so unhealthy. That lack of health is evident when nine out of ten churches are no longer reaching their communities.

But that can change. With you. Beginning now.

I am a church member.

In these next few pages, you can discover what that really means. Get ready for your life to change. Get ready for your church to change. And watch what an impact your church can have on the community and, indeed, the entire world.

Chapter 1

I Will Be a Functioning Church Member

It was a big deal for this young boy living in the small Southern town. I didn't know what a country club was, but I knew one was coming to town. And it included a swimming pool, a dining area, and meeting rooms. The owners also promised to build a small golf course, a promise they would fulfill a couple of years later.

Now don't get the wrong impression. This country club was not the typical upscale clubs we often envision. It was really a small private enterprise trying to make a few bucks in a small town by offering a few amenities.

But I was overwhelmed. My parents were middle-class in income, so they could afford the small monthly fee. From my perspective, though, I had it made. I could now go to a swimming pool. I didn't know of anyone who had their own pool in town, so this amenity was exciting. I could order a burger from the dining area. And we could have birthday parties in the pool or the meeting rooms.

I began to learn a lesson. Membership means perks. Membership means privileges. Membership means others will serve me. Just pay the going rate, and you can have others taking care of you while you enjoy a life of leisure.

And, tragically, this understanding of membership is what many church members hold.

"This is my church, so you have to play the music just the way I want it."

"Look pastor, you need to remember who pays your salary."

"If you don't do this program, I'll withhold my check to the church."

"I've been a member of this church for over thirty years, so I have a right to get what I want."

"I don't pay good money to this church to listen to sermons that long."

Okay, you get the picture. Those unfortunately typical comments come from members of churches who have an unbiblical view of membership. Their view of membership is more aligned with country club membership.

For them, membership is about receiving instead of giving, being served instead of serving, rights instead of responsibilities, and entitlements instead of sacrifices. This wrongful view of membership sees the tithes and offerings as membership dues that entitle members to a never-ending list of privileges and expectations, instead of an unconditional cheerful gift to God.

So, what does the Bible say about church membership?

I'm glad you asked.

Membership Means We Are All Necessary Parts of the Whole

There are a number of places in the New Testament where we can see a clear picture of church membership. One of the more voluminous sections is 1 Corinthians 12 to 14. In 1 Corinthians 12, Paul explains the metaphor of the church being a body with many members. In 1 Corinthians 13, he established love as the central attitude and action all members should have. And in 1 Corinthians 14, he returns to the messed-up church at Corinth that has the concept of membership all wrong.

Some church leaders and members view membership as a modern business or organizational concept, so they reject the label as unbiblical. Membership, to the contrary, is very biblical.

The Bible explains "members" differently than secular culture. For example, look at the term in 1 Corinthians 12:27–28: "Now you are the body of Christ, and individual members of it. And God has placed these in the church."

Do you get the difference? Members of a church comprise the whole and are essential parts of it. The apostle Paul would carry the body metaphor further and explain that members are individual parts of the body. Some are eyes; others are ears. Some are feet; still others are hands. That is why he concludes: "For as the body is one and has many parts, and all the parts of that body, though many are one body—so also is Christ" (1 Cor. 12:12).

Membership Means We Are Different but We Still Work Together

With a country club membership you pay others to do the work for you. With church membership, everyone has a role or function. That is why some are hands, feet, ears, or eyes. We are all different, but we are necessary parts of the whole.

Each part, therefore, has to do its work, or the whole body suffers. There is a beautiful diversity in the midst of unity in church membership. The Bible makes it clear that if one part does not do its job, the whole body does not function well. But if one part does its job well, the whole body rejoices and is stronger: "So if one member suffers, all the members suffer with it; if one member is honored, all the members rejoice with it" (1 Cor. 12:26).

Membership Means Everything We Say and Do Is Based on a Biblical Foundation of Love

Most Bible readers will speak glowingly of 1 Corinthians 13, commonly known as "the love chapter." It is read at weddings. It is used for a husband to declare his love for a wife, or vice versa. It is preached to demonstrate a fuller meaning of *agape* or unconditional love.

While there is nothing wrong with using the love chapter in these contexts, its original meaning was to demonstrate how church members relate one to another. Can you imagine 1 Corinthians 13 being read at an acrimonious church meeting? In its full biblical context that might be the best place to read it.

If we could just abide by the principles of the love chapter, we would have completely healthy churches. It would be a revolution!

Just look at some of the relational principles of 1 Corinthians 13: "Love is patient, love is kind. Love does not envy, is not boastful, is not conceited, does not act improperly, is not selfish, is not provoked, and does not keep a record of wrongs" (vv. 4–5).

The principles of these two verses alone are sufficient to cause a revival in most churches!

We are not to love fellow church members just because they are lovable. We are to love the unlovable as well. We are not to pray for and encourage our pastors just when they are doing things we like. We are to pray for and encourage them when they do things we don't like. We are not to serve the church only when others are joining in. We are to serve the church even if we are alone in doing so.

Church membership is founded on love. Authentic, biblical, unconditional love.

Church Membership Is Functioning Membership

Do you know how to remain a member of a country club? Pay your dues. Do that and people will be available to serve you.

Do you know how to remain a *biblical* member of a church? Give abundantly and serve without hesitation.

Note the italicized word: *biblical*. Sure, you can remain on the rolls of many churches and never show up or give. You can remain an "active" member in other churches by being a CEO Christian: Christmas and Easter Only. You can even be a revered member in a number of churches by giving a nice sum to the church each year, even though you never lift a finger in service or ministry.

But please understand. That type of membership is not biblical membership. That approach to membership is man-made, man-centered, and man-maintained. It is totally contrary to what the Bible teaches. It has no place in our churches.

Biblical church membership gives without qualification. Biblical membership views the tithes and offerings as joyous giving. There are no strings attached. Biblical church membership serves and ministers as a natural way of doing things.

Biblical church membership is *functioning* membership.

Again, let's return to 1 Corinthians 12 to grasp this concept more fully. When Paul was using the metaphor of the body to speak of the church, he did so for two primary reasons. First, the body is a unified whole. Likewise, the church is to be unified in its mission, purposes, ministries, and activities.

Second, the body is not only unified, it is made up of many parts. Think about the parts noted in 1 Corinthians 12:12–26:

- The foot.
- The hand.
- The ear.
- The eye.
- The nose (at least indirectly by referring to the sense of smell).

Each of these parts is supposed to function. The foot is to walk. The hand is to grasp and hold. The ear is to hear. The eye is to see. The nose is to smell.

We who are church members are all supposed to function in the church. The concept of an inactive church member is an oxymoron. Biblically, no such church member really exists.

Such is the reason we are exhorted to know our gifts and abilities, so we can use them best to serve the church for the glory of God. The fact that there is so much diversity in our church is our strength. Everyone has a function. Everyone should be functioning. Everyone should have a role.

Because we are all different with different gifts and abilities, we will function differently from other members. But if we are true and biblical church members, we will be functioning members.

One of the ongoing questions you should ask yourself and God in prayer is: "How can I best serve my church?" You should never ask yourself if you *should* be serving your church.

If you are a member, you must be a functioning member. It's just that simple.

The First Pledge

It's hard to know for certain. Church membership rolls are not always easy to research, and some churches just refuse to face reality. But, by our best estimates, we think most church rolls are overinflated by a factor of three.

That's big. Really big.

What that means is, if your church has three hundred members on its rolls, it probably only has a hundred real biblical members. Only one-third are functioning members. Only one out of three gives abundantly and serves without hesitation.

In fact, I bet many people will question our own numbers as being overstated. They will question if *as many* as one out of three members are biblical, functioning members.

But you are making a different commitment.

You are making a pledge to be a member the way the Bible speaks and the way God designed it.

You are committing to giving cheerfully and abundantly. You are committing to serving and ministering without hesitation.

You are pledging to be a functioning church member.

The First Pledge
I am a church member.

I like the metaphor of membership. It's not membership as in a civic organization or a country club. It's the kind of membership given to us in 1 Corinthians 12: "Now you are the body of Christ, and individual members of it" (1 Cor. 12:27). Because I am a member of the body of Christ, I must be a functioning member, whether I am an "eye," an "ear," or a "hand." As a functioning member, I will give. I will serve. I will minister. I will evangelize. I will study. I will seek to be a blessing to others. I will remember that "if one member suffers, all the members suffer with it; if one member is honored, all the members rejoice with it" (1 Cor. 12:26).

Sign and Date

Questions for Study

1. Explain how country club membership and church membership are so different. Give scriptural references to support the differences in church membership.

2. Explain why church membership is a biblical concept, using 1 Corinthians 12 as your biblical foundation.

3. How is the "love chapter," 1 Corinthians 13, related to church membership? Explain using all 13 verses of the chapter.

4. How are the different parts of the body (ear, nose, mouth, hand, foot, eyes, etc.) related to church membership? How do the parts play out in your church?

5. In relation to church membership, why is it important for members to know and use their spiritual gifts? Relate your answer to 1 Corinthians 12.

Chapter 2

I Will Be a Unifying Church Member

God desires for Christians to get along. In fact He is emphatic about it. Jesus was clear when He said: "By this all people will know that you are My disciples, if you have love for one another" (John 13:35).

Did you get that?

The world will know if we are Christians or not by the way we who are believers act toward one another. Have you ever been to an ugly business meeting in a church? Do you think an outsider would have been impressed with the "Christian" behavior she witnessed?

Have you ever heard Christians gossip about other Christians? Is that loving one another?

Look at your pastor's e-mail inbox if he'll let you. I bet some of you would be shocked by what some church members say to him.

When you become a Christian, God expects you to be a part of His church. But when you become a part of His church, He wants you to be a unifying presence there. Let's state that a bit more strongly. He *demands* that you become a unifying presence there.

The evidence is pretty clear. Let's take a look.

That Thing Called Unity

I love team sports. I've seen teams with only average talent win championships. Don't get me wrong; talent and gifted athletes are important. But what is even more important is how those athletes work together. Unity is important. Unity is critical.

Likewise, when church members don't work together, the church is weaker as a whole. My analogy may be weak because the local church is much more important than any sports team. But I hope you get the point. Unity is vital to the health of a church. And that means every church member, you and I included, must contribute to the unity of the church.

The apostle Paul said a lot about unity when he wrote his letter to the Ephesians. Paul obviously liked the church at Ephesus. Look at some of his words he wrote to the church: "This is why, since I heard about your faith in the Lord Jesus and your love for all the saints, I never stop giving thanks for you as I remember you in my prayers" (Eph. 1:15–16).

Did you pick up on why Paul was thankful for those church members? He was thankful for their faith in Jesus and, get this, for *"your love for all the saints."* We sometimes call a real godly person a saint, but in the Bible it simply refers to Christians. So Paul was thankful because these church members were showing love for one another.

Unity is critically important.

Paul would emphasize it again to the church members at Ephesus. He urged the members "to walk worthy of the calling you have received, with all humility and gentleness, with patience, accepting one another in love, *diligently keeping the unity of the Spirit* with the peace that binds us" (Eph. 4:1–3, emphasis added).

You have a responsibility as a church member. You are to be a source of unity. You are never to be a divisive force. You are to love your fellow church members unconditionally. And while that doesn't mean you agree with everyone all the time, it does mean you are willing to sacrifice your own preferences to keep unity in your church.

But we will get to that issue of preferences later.

For now the issue is unity. For when we seek unity, we demonstrate love. Look at Paul's words one more time, this time in his letter to the church at Colossae: "Above all, put on love—the perfect bond of unity" (Col. 3:14).

Paul said "above all." It doesn't get much more important than that.

Unity is really important in your church. Are you doing your part?

Gossip and Other Negative Talk

Romans 1:29–31 is pretty depressing. It's a listing of many unrighteous acts: "They are filled with all unrighteousness, evil, greed, and wickedness. They are full of envy, murder, quarrels, deceit, and malice. They are gossips, slanderers, God-haters, arrogant, proud, boastful, inventors of evil, disobedient to parents, undiscerning, untrustworthy, unloving, and unmerciful."

Whew. That list will wear you out. And right in the middle of it is the evil deed of gossip. The simple dictionary meaning of *gossip* speaks volume. Some dictionaries call it "idle talk."

Some connect it to rumors. Others say it's unproven personal or private information about others.

Gossip is bad. And gossip is destructive in your church.

This chapter is about unity. And few things can destroy the unity of a church like gossip. A unified church is powerful. Gossip tears apart that unity and renders a church powerless.

One of my friends who leads a well-known Christian organization told me that the prohibition of gossip is actually spelled out in the employee policy manual. If an employee has a concern about another employee, he or she is supposed to take that concern directly to the employee. If, for any reason, the concern can't be presented directly, the employee must go to his or her supervisor.

Gossip is not tolerated. An employee can even lose his job over it. Why? Because it tears down the unity in the organization.

James minced no words when he wrote about the negative power of the tongue: "And the tongue is a fire. The tongue, a world of unrighteousness, is placed among the parts of our bodies. It pollutes the whole body, sets the course of life on fire, and is set on fire by hell" (James 3:6).

So how should we respond to this issue of gossip in our church? First, don't be a source of gossip. If you have any doubt whether something is gossip or not, don't mention it. Keep your tongue under control.

Second, if someone in the church begins to share gossip with you, gently rebuke him or her. You don't have to be harsh in your response to them. Kindly say that you would rather not hear any gossip and you would hope it wouldn't continue to spread. You can be a unifier in your church with those simple words.

And if there are just a few more members like you, word will begin to travel. Other church members will know that gossip is not tolerated in your church. And the congregation will be a place of joy and unity.

"For the one who wants to love life and to see good days must keep his tongue from evil and his lips from speaking deceit" (1 Pet. 3:10).

Love life. See good days. Control your tongue. Stop the gossip. Be a unifier.

Forgiveness and Unity

It was one of those experiences that seemed to come out of left field. I was a young man in the business world. My wife and I had joined a church that we loved. We loved the pastor and his preaching. We loved the fellowship. We loved the ministries of the church.

My pastor mentioned in a sermon that he would be willing to meet with any men on Tuesday morning at 5:00 a.m. to pray for God's leadership in the church. He said he wasn't looking for a crowd—just a few men that wanted to make the commitment. I jumped at the opportunity.

Those mornings are memories I covet to this day, more than three decades later. Praying with godly men. Fellowship with a pastor I loved. Seeing God really move in our lives.

Then it happened.

We began our prayer time with no words spoken aloud. We were taking time to talk to God before we verbalized our prayers for others to hear. But every time I tried to pray, my mind went back to my high school years. Every time, the teacher's face would appear in my mind's eye. It was so strange but I couldn't pray.

You see, the teacher had physically abused me. I had kept the secret and told no one. I was ashamed, angry, and . . . unforgiving. I realized what God was doing. If God was to use me as His instrument in the church, I had to forgive the teacher. So I told my fellow prayer warriors and asked God to forgive me for the sin of not forgiving. Then I forgave the man who had hurt me many years earlier.

The moment was liberating. My prayer life opened again. And God began to use me in unexpected ways. I would soon leave the church and my business job. God called me to vocational ministry. And it all began with forgiveness.

Jesus said it clearly: "For if you forgive people their wrongdoing, your heavenly Father will forgive you as well. But if you don't forgive people, your Father will not forgive your wrongdoing" (Matt. 6:14–15).

Unity in the church will not happen if members have unforgiving hearts. Too many times members have anger and hurt because of something another member has said or done. Some members are angry and hurt at the pastor and staff because of something they said or did or failed to do.

I love the way Paul put it in Colossians 3:12–13, as he spoke directly to the members of the church: "Therefore, God's chosen ones, holy and loved, put on heartfelt compassion, kindness, humility, gentleness, and patience, accepting one another and forgiving one another if anyone has a complaint against another. Just as the Lord has forgiven you, so you must also forgive."

Each local church is made up of imperfect members and imperfect pastors. We will make mistakes. We will all sin. Yes, we are all hypocrites.

Church unity is torn apart when members refuse to forgive, when any member is too prideful to grant forgiveness.

Remember, Christ loved us so much that He died on a cross to forgive us. And now, as He has forgiven us, so we must forgive others.

It is essential to the unity of your church.

The Second Pledge

Even at this early part of the book, I hope you see church membership is more than getting your name on a roll. It's different from the perks and privileges you have when you are in a social club. To the contrary, church membership is about sacrificing, giving, and forgiving.

This is the second of six pledges in this book. Before you make the pledge, think carefully about the words you will read. Think especially carefully about the words in the Bible about church unity. And pray before and after you make the pledge. Seek God's strength to help you keep this pledge.

The Second Pledge
I am a church member.

   I will seek to be a source of unity in my church. I know there are no perfect pastors, staff, or other church members. But neither am I. I will not be a source of gossip or dissension. One of the greatest contributions I can make is to do all I can in God's power to help keep the church in unity for the sake of the gospel.

_____

Sign and Date

Questions for Study

1. What did Paul mean when he said in Colossians 3:14 that love is the perfect bond of unity? What does that mean for the local church today?

2. What is the best path to take if someone brings gossip to you in your church? What does the Bible say about gossip?

3. How is forgiveness related to unity in the local church? What does the Bible say about forgiving one another?

4. Look at Matthew 6:14–15. Relate those words to being a church member. What does it mean if one church member does not forgive another?

5. Read all of 1 Corinthians 13. Paul wrote the "love chapter" to the church at Corinth where problems with unity were pervasive. What does this chapter mean for church members today? Explain as you go through each verse.

Chapter 3

I Will Not Let My Church Be about My Preferences and Desires

Often I'm tempted to use illustrations of my children in a various settings since I have such a love for my three sons. Even now that they are adults with their own children, I sometimes find myself talking about them when they were little boys.

So I thought I might begin this chapter by giving an illustration about my boys fussing and fighting because they wanted something their way. But then I begin to think how many times I fought with my own older brother because I wanted it my way, right now, without compromise.

I could be a selfish brat. It's good we grow out of that phase after we become adults. Right? It's even better that we never revert to that phase after we become Christians. Right?

Wrong!

Christians can sometimes act just like those demanding children who want things their way. Temper tantrums in churches may not include church members lying on the floor kicking and screaming, but some come close.

But the strange thing about church membership is that you actually give up your preferences when you join. Don't get me wrong; there may be much about your church that you like a lot. But you are there to meet the needs of others. You are there to serve others. You are there to give. You are there to sacrifice.

Get the picture?

Jesus would often say things that confounded His listeners. You see, even His disciples had a tendency to fight with one another. On one occasion the Twelve were arguing about who was the greatest. Can you imagine that? The closest followers of Jesus were having a "me first" fight. The Bible says that Jesus stopped and sat down and called these grown men together. "Sitting down, He called the Twelve and said to them, 'If anyone wants to be first, he must be last of all and servant of all'" (Mark 9:35).

Ouch.

I would have loved to have been a fly on a cloak and seen their expressions. Yep, He got you this time, you self-serving disciples.

And then it hits me. That text is for me as well. As a church member, my motivation should not be to get my preferences to the top of the list. I am supposed to be last, not first. I am supposed to be a servant instead of seeking to be served.

Okay, let's dig a little deeper into what it means to be a servant.

The Servant Motif

The word *servant* occurs fifty-seven times in the New Testament. Sometimes it refers to a person who has that official role in a household. But many times it refers to the role we are to assume as Christians. Also, *serve* occurs fifty-eight times in the New Testament.

Get the picture? Serving is important in the Bible.

Jesus said we must be last of all and servant of all. That doesn't sound like all the church members we may know. Many church members demand their preferences, their desires, and the way they've always done it.

But Jesus said we are to serve.

Paul said it as well. After he became a Christian, the apostle declared, "I was made a servant of this gospel by the gift of God's grace that was given to me by the working of His power" (Eph. 3:7).

We will never find joy in church membership when we are constantly seeking things our way. But paradoxically, we will find the greatest joy when we choose to be last. That's what Jesus meant when He said the last will be first. True joy means giving up our rights and preferences and serving everyone else.

And that's what church membership means as well.

A Survey That Said a Lot

My research team recently conducted a survey of churches that were inwardly focused. For the most part, they were not serving past their own walls and their own members. In other words, these churches were largely self-serving.

In our survey we found ten dominant behavior patterns of members in these churches. See if you recognize any:

1. **Worship wars.** One or more factions in the church want the music just the way they like it. Any deviation is met with anger and demands for change. The order of service must remain constant. Certain instrumentation is required while others are prohibited.

2. **Prolonged minutia meetings.** The church spends an inordinate amount of time in different meetings. Most of the meetings deal with the most inconsequential items, while the Great Commission and Great Commandment are rarely the topics of discussion.

3. **Facility focus.** The church facilities develop iconic status. One of the highest priorities in the church is the protection and preservation of rooms, furniture, and other visible parts of the church's buildings and grounds.

4. **Program driven.** Every church has programs even if they don't admit it. When we start doing a ministry a certain way, it takes on programmatic status. The problem is not with programs. The problem develops when the program becomes an end instead of a means to greater ministry.

5. **Inwardly focused budget.** A disproportionate share of the budget is used to meet the needs and comforts of the members instead of reaching beyond the walls of the church.

6. **Inordinate demands for pastoral care.** All church members deserve care and concern, especially in times of need and crisis. Problems develop, however, when church members have unreasonable expectations for even minor matters. Some members expect the pastoral

staff to visit them regularly merely because they have membership status.

7. **Attitudes of entitlement.** This issue could be a catch-all for many of the points named here. The overarching attitude is one of demanding and having a sense of deserving special treatment.

8. **Greater concern about change than the gospel.** Almost any noticeable changes in the church evoke the ire of many; but those same passions are not evident about participating in the work of the gospel to change lives.

9. **Anger and hostility.** Members are consistently angry. They regularly express hostility toward the church staff and other members.

10. **Evangelistic apathy.** Very few members share their faith on a regular basis. More are concerned about their own needs rather than the greatest eternal needs of the world and community in which they live.

In almost every behavior above, church members were looking out for their own needs and preferences. I want the music my way. I want the building my way. I am upset because the pastor didn't visit me. I don't want to change anything in my church.

You get the picture. I. Me. Myself.

Church membership from a biblical perspective, however, is about servanthood. It's about giving. It's about putting others first.

The Mind of Christ

One of the best descriptions of the attitude we should embody was written by Paul in Philippians 2:5–11. The apostle says cogently and powerfully, "Make your own attitude that of Christ Jesus." So what did Jesus do?

- He "did not consider equality with God as something to be used for His own advantage."
- "He emptied Himself by assuming the form of a slave."
- "He humbled Himself."
- He became "obedient to the point of death—even to death on a cross."

Keep in mind that Philippians 2 is not only a description of the obedience of Christ; it is an example for us to follow. We are to be servants. We are to be obedient. We are to put others first. We are to do whatever it takes to keep the unity in our church.

So if we approach church membership from the perspective of entitlement, we have it upside down. You always ask first what you can do for your church.

Then you will have discovered the joy of being last.

The Third Pledge

Typically it's easier to sign a commitment on paper than it is to practice that commitment in reality. You need a fair warning before you take this third step. It won't be long after making this commitment that you will come across a fellow church member whose attitude is, well, nothing like the attitude of Christ. She will tell you what's wrong with the music or the preaching or the pastor, you name it.

It will be tempting to chew her out, to tell her to let go of her lousy attitude. And while a gentle rebuke may be in order, you need to remember something about your commitment. This cantankerous and ornery church member is one of those you have pledged to serve.

My point is that these commitments are not easy. In fact, without God's power they may prove impossible. So pray for His strength and His wisdom. And when you think you've had it with making sacrifices for others, remember the cross. As you are overwhelmed by Jesus' undeserved love for you that caused Him to sacrifice everything—including His preferences—you will be able to do the same for others.

That will put things in perspective.

The Third Pledge
I am a church member.

I will not let my church be about my preferences and desires. That is self-serving. I am a member in this church to serve others and to serve Christ. My Savior went to a cross for me. I can deal with any inconveniences and matters that just aren't my preference or style.

_____

Sign and Date

Questions for Study

1. Show from key Bible verses the difference between church membership and country club membership from the perspective of personal preferences and desires. Of course, the Bible doesn't speak of country club membership, so you will need to assume the benefits of belonging to one.

2. Find and explain key passages in the Bible that talk about Christians being like servants. How would you describe a servant as it applies to being a member of a church?

3. Why do many churches have "worship wars"? What does that have to do with the right or wrong attitude about church membership?

4. Describe someone in your church that best fits the description of having the mind of Christ and a servant attitude. Find key New Testament passages that would fit him or her.

5. Go verse by verse through Philippians 2:5–11. Explain how the attitude of Christ in each verse becomes a pattern for us as church members.

Chapter 4

I Will Pray for My Church Leaders

It's Thursday morning. Pastor Mike has a clear calendar, an aberration in his busy schedule. Actually, the calendar is not really clear. He has set aside time to finish his sermon for Sunday. His Bible is open. Study aids are nearby. He begins to study.

Then the phone rings.

His assistant tells him about a car accident involving a family in the church. The ambulances are already on the way to the hospital. Mike leaves all his study material on his desk and jumps into the car.

On the way to the hospital, his assistant calls him again. The entire Godsey family of five were in the car. None are seriously hurt except Gary, the father and husband of the family. His condition is grave.

Pastor Mike walks into the emergency room. The family has just been told that their husband and father did not make it. They see their pastor and run to him sobbing, in total shock. Mike is there for them. He stays with the entire family for three hours until he is certain enough people are around to care for them.

He stops by his home to see his wife and grab a quick sandwich. It is now afternoon. He's not sure if he can return to his sermon preparation, but he knows he must. He must fight the emotional exhaustion of the morning and finish the message. But as he walks back to the church, his assistant apologetically tells him that two people need to speak with him. They consider it urgent.

Mike meets with the two men. One of them is the worship leader of the church. He is struggling with his ministry and is considering giving up. For two hours Mike listens, consoles, and attempts to encourage the staff member.

The next visitor then catches Mike off guard. George is one of the key lay leaders in the church. Mike considers him a friend and an incredibly vital person in the overall leadership of the congregation. George struggles to speak: "My wife is having an affair . . ." There are no more words for five minutes. Just tears and sobs.

Mike stays with George for over two hours. They pray together and talk about next steps.

It's nearly five o'clock in the afternoon. Mike is too drained to attempt to get back to his sermon. Instead he begins to look at his crowded e-mail inbox. He cringes when he sees one of the senders of an e-mail. But he cannot stop himself from opening the message. It's from one of Mike's most frequent critics in the church. She has two complaints. The first irritation was something he said in last Sunday's sermon. The second complaint addressed Mike's failure to visit her sister-in-law who had minor outpatient surgery yesterday. The woman is not a member of the church. And Mike knew nothing about the surgery.

Pastor Mike shuts the laptop cover and moves to his car slowly. He'll stop by the house to grab a quick bite to eat. Then he needs to check on the Godsey family. He will stay with them for a while, but he must leave prior to 7:30, when he is to give the invocation for a local high school basketball game.

Several people corner him at the game, so he doesn't get home until after nine o'clock. He goes to his small study in his home, shuts the door, and begins to cry.

Gary Godsey, the father and husband who was killed in the car accident, was Mike's best friend.

This was the first chance Mike had to grieve.

Pray for the Pastor and Other Church Leaders

All church leaders need prayer. I will usually say "pastor," but that can mean minister or elder or director or whatever term you use. It may refer to the senior leader, or it could be about someone else on staff. The point is that we church members must pray for our church leaders.

The previous story is true; all I did was change some names. Such is the life of a pastor. His day is filled with mountaintops and valleys. He is adulated by some and castigated by others. He needs our prayers.

He certainly needs our prayers for his sermons. We should pray that God would give him the wisdom, insight, and words to preach. It is an incredible task to speak and preach the Word of God every week again and again. There are those who will be listening to the preacher, but they need to hear from God.

Pray for his preaching.

Pray for Him and His Family

One of the most convicting and challenging verses for pastors is 1 Timothy 3:5: "If anyone does not know how to manage his own household, how will he take care of God's church?" I have heard countless pastors worry about and struggle over their families.

They worry that they neglect their families because of the demands of the church.

They worry about their families living in a glass house.

They anguish when critics direct barbs at family members.

You get the picture.

We are church members. We must be the prayer intercessors for pastors and their families. Few families face the kinds of pressures and expectations as the families of pastors.

Pray for the pastor's family.

Pray for His Protection

Read these words from the Bible about the qualifications of the pastor (overseer). These words are not exhaustive. There are other passages regarding his qualifications. From 1 Timothy 3:2–4: "An overseer, therefore, must be above reproach, the husband of one wife, self-controlled, sensible, respectable, hospitable, an able teacher, not addicted to wine, not a bully but gentle, not quarrelsome, not greedy—one who manages his own household competently, having his children under control with all dignity."

Whew.

Just to get past "the above reproach" part is an accomplishment! The word *reproach* means "to find fault." So to be "above reproach" means to be above finding fault. While the pastor is certainly not expected to be perfect, he is to have a reputation above most everyone else. When people in the community speak or think about the pastor, the thoughts and words should be positive and encouraging.

That's quite an expectation to hold. On top of that, the pastor must maintain good self-control. He must be sensible, respectable, and hospitable. He must be a good teacher. He must be gentle and not argumentative. He must not be greedy. And, to add just a little more pressure, his family must reflect a healthy, Christian family.

Do you see why we church members must pray for the pastor's protection?

In that list of the qualifications of a pastor in 1 Timothy 3, the seventh verse puts it all into perspective: "Furthermore, he must have a good reputation among outsiders, so that he does not fall into disgrace and the devil's trap."

The "outsiders" in that verse refers to the unbelievers who are not a part of the church. In that context the verse mentions "the devil's trap." Let's not move past those words too quickly. "The devil" is obvious. He is the literal chief among all demons. He is real. He is powerful.

But, in a rare use of the word, the verse speaks of the devil's "trap." If we understand the full implications of that word, we wouldn't hesitate to pray for our pastor's protection. A trap is something that is set intentionally. It means that the devil has devised a plan to bring the pastor down. He has set a trap.

It means that the devil sees the pastor as a threat, and one of his highest priorities is to take him down and take him out. And the text is clear. The nature of this trap will be temptation where the pastor's reputation will be harmed.

We should not be surprised, then, when we hear about a pastor's moral failure. We are grieved and heartbroken, but not surprised. The devil is setting traps for pastors—anything he can do to bring harm to the pastor's reputation. He will stop at nothing—greed, adultery, anger, addiction—to catch the pastor in his trap.

The devil is powerful. But God is so much more powerful.

And God, in ways we don't always understand fully, works through the prayers of believers.

We are church members. We will pray for the protection of our pastor and other church leaders. We will do all we can through prayer to keep our pastor out of the devil's trap.

Pray for His Physical and Mental Health

Serving and leading a church well expends all of a pastor's energy. He is on call every day and every hour. Because the demands are so great on him, the pastor often neglects his own health and well-being.

While no one is invulnerable to sickness and accidents, we can pray for the protection of our pastor's health.

We should also pray for our pastor's mental health. In this regard I'm not referring to the opposite of mental sickness as I am to wisdom. The pastor has to make dozens of decisions each week that require discernment and wisdom. He needs wisdom to know what to preach and teach and how to present God's Word. He needs wisdom dealing with us church members each week so he can best discern how to respond to the plethora of demands upon him.

We who are church members should pray for the health of our pastor. He will feel stress and pressure every day. We can pray that he will experience the peace that only God can give.

The Fourth Pledge

This pledge requires discipline, but it does not necessarily require a lot of time. In fact, I have been asking church members for years to pray five minutes a day for their pastors. Some started praying for their pastors first thing in the morning. Others wove it into their work schedule, during breaks or lunch. Still others prayed for their pastors with their spouses in the evening.

As church members, we must be willing to pray for the leaders in our church. Without our ongoing intercessory prayer, our churches will not be healthy.

Five minutes a day. That is all. Sure, you can pray longer if you like. Frances Mason, who is in heaven now, prayed for me an hour a day when I was a pastor. But you can start with five minutes. Will you pray five minutes every day for the leaders in your church?

The Fourth Pledge
I am a church member.

I will pray for my pastor every day. I understand that the pastor's work is never ending. His days are filled with numerous demands that bring emotional highs and lows. He must deal with critics. He must be a good husband and father. Because my pastor cannot do all things in his own power, I will pray for his strength and wisdom daily.

_____

Sign and Date

Questions for Study

1. Using scriptural backing, explain why the pastor's family is such an important factor in his ministry.

2. What is meant by "above reproach" in 1 Timothy 3:2? Is that standard even possible for the pastor?

3. Explain the implications of the devil's trap in 1 Timothy 3:7.

4. What is the meaning of "outsiders" in 1 Timothy 3:7? Why should they be a concern to church members or pastors?

5. Find some key passages in the Bible where intercessory prayer takes place (someone praying for someone else). Relate those passages to praying for your pastor.

Chapter 5

I Will Lead My Family to Be Healthy Church Members

His name was Bob.

He died a few years ago, but, if he influenced just a few people like he influenced me, this relatively unknown and quiet man changed the world.

Bob always seemed to be at the church. I understand that some people show up at church every time the doors are open out of guilt or legalistic obligation. Not Bob. He was always joyous, always serving, always kind. You could just tell he loved serving the church.

The same could be said about Bob's wife and two sons. They too seemed to love the church and to find joy in serving. The whole family was, well, different. But different in a good kind of way, if you know what I mean.

I was a young businessman in my early twenties. I had been married for three years and had just become a dad. Fatherhood hit me like a ton of bricks. I wanted to be a good husband and a good dad. And that meant getting involved at church. Really involved.

I didn't know it at the time, but Bob was watching me. He was concerned for me. He loved my youthful enthusiasm, but he knew what was coming. The more I got involved, the more I would see the imperfections of the church, the pastor, the staff, and other church members. Bob had seen the pattern repeatedly. Get excited about church. Get more involved. Discover the imperfections of the church. Get discouraged about the church. Leave the church.

Bob took me under his wing. When I would begin to get angry, frustrated, or discouraged about something at the church, he would talk to me. He would explain that no church is perfect. No pastor is perfect. No church member is perfect. And he would gently remind me that I was not close to perfect either.

He told me that we were to find joy in serving the church and those in the church. We were not a part of the church to see what we could get out of it. We were a part of the church to serve and care for others. Our perspective should always be on giving, not receiving. And if someone did something that disappointed or frustrated us, that was God's way of telling us to pray for that person.

Bob told me that we could never have the perfection of Christ but that we could strive to be more like Him. He reminded me that Christ died on the cross for people who rebelled against Him. We should be able, therefore, to love the seemingly unlovable at our church.

Through Bob's patient biblical teaching, I learned to love the local church. I learned to love the people despite their imperfections. Bob would teach me to look at the "log" in my eye (my own imperfections) before I judged the "speck" in other's eyes (Matt. 7:3–5).

I wish my own parents had taught me how to love the local church. But Bob was a good spiritual father to me.

By the way, Bob's two sons are grown men now. And it's no surprise. They are serving and loving their local churches just like their dad.

After all, he taught them well.

Church and Family

It's no surprise that we are taught in Scripture that families are analogous to the church. Paul wrote these words in Ephesians 5:22–26: "Wives, submit to your own husbands as to the Lord, for the husband is the head of the wife as Christ is the head of the church. He is the Savior of the body. Now as the church submits to Christ, so wives are to submit to their husbands in everything. Husbands, love your wives, just as Christ loved the church and gave Himself for her to make her holy, cleansing her with the washing of water by the word."

Paul would then make clear the relationship between the church and the family in verses 32–33: "This mystery is profound, but I am talking about Christ and the church. To sum up, each one of you is to love his wife as himself, and the wife is to respect her husband."

The biblical text continues in Ephesians 6:1–4, but this time the subject is parents and children: "Children, obey your parents as you would the Lord, because this is right. Honor your father and mother, which is the first commandment with a promise, so that it may go well with you and that you may have a long life in the land. Fathers, don't stir up anger in your children, but bring them up in the training and instruction of the Lord."

These passages remind us that, just as we are supposed to sacrifice and love our families unconditionally, so are we to love those churches where God has placed us. Our family members are not perfect, and neither are the members of the church. We are to find our joy in serving both our families and the church.

We are further reminded of the importance of the family to the church. We are to encourage our family members to be faithful to the church. We should pray together as family members for our churches. Indeed, as we are to strive to love our families more deeply, so should we exhort our family members to love the church more deeply.

Praying Together as a Family for the Church

One of the many lessons I learned from Bob was to bring my family together to pray for my church. Following Bob's leadership, I would learn to pray for the leadership of the church in a number of ways:

- For spiritual protection.
- For protection from moral failure.
- For the preaching of the Word.
- For their families.
- For encouragement.

- For physical strength.
- For courage.
- For discernment.
- For wisdom in their leadership.

As my family grew, we would follow the pattern that Bob taught me. As our family prayed together for our church, my three sons grew up with a love for the church. They were not blind to the problems and challenges that occur in any church. They did learn, however, to love people unconditionally. And in doing so they learned to love the church.

Part of the opportunity and honor of being a church member is the teaching of our family to love the church. And that teaching often begins by praying together as a family for the church where God placed us.

Worshipping Together as a Family

As a church member, I am responsible for encouraging and leading my entire family to worship together in the church. If I am married, I seek to include my spouse. If I am a parent, I seek to include my children. My family must see my love for the church.

Many church members are single. They have no immediate family with whom they can worship in the church. Regardless, there are still people watching them and how they love the church. They are to be an example to others.

The situation is especially poignant when a church member has a family member who is not a Christian or part of the church. The apostle Paul addressed the issue of divorce and separation in 1 Corinthians 7. In essence, he instructed that the believing spouse should never take the initiative to leave the unbelieving spouse (vv. 10–13).

Paul then explains one of the primary reasons for the admonition: the believing spouse is a testimony of Christ to the unbelieving spouse and to any children in the family. Look at his words in 1 Corinthians 7:14: "For the unbelieving husband is set apart for God by the wife, and the unbelieving wife is set apart for God by the husband. Otherwise your children would be corrupt, but now they are set apart for God."

It can be lonely to be the believer in an unbelieving family. It can likewise be lonely going to worship at your church alone, while your spouse remains behind. But God has given such people a mission field: their families. Like the missionary who travels thousands of miles to tell the good news to unevangelized people, this church member is to tell the good news in his or her own home.

More times than not, the believing spouse is the wife. Whether she knows it or not, her husband is watching her closely.

How that wife responds to her husband impacts her witness. And how that wife loves her church and those within the church affects her husband. A godly spouse can be a key factor in the unbelieving spouse coming to Christ. And that godliness is often demonstrated by the believing spouse's love of the church.

Falling Deeply in Love with the Bride of Christ

As a church member, I am not merely to like my church or serve my church well. I am to fall deeply in love with my church. Christ is the bridegroom, and the church is the bride. My commitment is to love that bride with an unwavering and unconditional love.

Unconditional love is not always easy. If someone is perfect and meets our every perceived need, it's easy to think we love that person. But such love is one-way. It's all about me and my needs. Unconditional love means I will continue to fall more deeply in love regardless of the response. It means my love for the church will grow even as I may disagree with something or encounter disagreeable people.

And as I grow more deeply in love with my church, I will do all I can in God's power to bring my family with me. We will pray for our church leaders together. We will worship together. And we will serve together.

If our family gets discouraged or discontent in our church, we will remind ourselves that unconditional love is not always easy. But we will also remind ourselves that unconditional love has been demonstrated perfectly for us. His name is Jesus. He loves us, sins and all, so much that He died on a cross for us.

"But God proves His own love for us in that while we were still sinners, Christ died for us" (Rom. 5:8).

The Fifth Pledge

The church is a family.

We have our own families as well; some are healthier than others. The fifth commitment recognizes the importance of the immediate family supporting and loving the church family.

The fifth pledge is a commitment to unite your family in love for your church. If your family members are believers who are a part of the church, then you should seek to pray together for the church and to worship together. If there are unbelievers in your family, then you should seek to demonstrate a deep love for Christ's church. Such love can influence them and move them closer to Christ. If you are a single person living alone, then you can be assured that others are watching you. How you love your church could have a significant spiritual impact on their lives.

The Fifth Pledge
I am a church member.

I will lead my family to be good members of this church as well. We will pray together for our church. We will worship together in our church. We will serve together in our church. And we will ask Christ to help us fall deeper in love with this church because He gave His life for her.

_____
Sign and Date

Questions for Study

1. How does the biblical teaching of the log and the speck in Matthew 7 apply to church membership?

2. What is the relationship of our immediate families and the church family? What biblical texts make this connection?

3. What is the role of a believing spouse to an unbelieving spouse? How does that manifest itself in church membership?

4. Why is unconditional love such a challenge, especially as it applies to church membership?

5. How is Christ's death on the cross an example for us as church members relating to one another?

Chapter 6

I Will Treasure Church Membership as a Gift

Imagine a child facing two scenarios. In the first scenario mom tells "Johnny" that he must clean his room. It must be spotless. He will probably have to put hours into his efforts. Anything less than perfection is not acceptable. Whether he likes it or not, that room must be cleaner than it has ever been before.

In the second scenario mom tells Johnny that someone has given him an incredible gift. It is wrapped and ready to open. She increases his excitement by letting him know this gift will be one of the greatest he has received or ever will receive. It will bring him countless hours of joy.

Okay, if Johnny has the choice of scenario one or scenario two, which does he choose?

Duh.

Okay, I know the two scenarios are unlikely. And I know the choice is obvious.

But every church member faces two distinct scenarios where the choice is just as obvious.

In the first option we approach church membership similar to country club membership noted in chapter one. We are joining the church to see what we can get out of it. The pastor is to feed us through his sermons. We have specified an acceptable range for the length of the sermon. The music is to fit our style exactly. Any deviations are not acceptable. The programs and ministries are for our benefit. We will determine what we like and don't like. We are members who expect perks, privileges, and service.

So what happens when the country club church member is asked to contribute to the work of the church? What happens if such a member is asked to serve in the nursery for a few weeks? What happens if that member is asked to lead a fifth-grade boys' Bible study class?

The response is predictable. One country club member may agree to the request out of obligation. She has a legalistic approach to serving. It's not that she wants to do it. After all, country club church membership is not about working; it's about being served. But since she's been asked, she begrudgingly accepts and begins the ministry with a bad attitude.

She won't last long.

Other country club church members just get mad when they are asked. Some may respond that they did their time in earlier years. They make ministry sound like a prison sentence. Still some refuse to offer a reason why they won't contribute; they are simply indignant that they were asked. And yet another group of country club church members gets angry toward the pastors. After all, that's what we pay them to do. Those pastors are just lazy, trying to get out of work.

But there is a second option to church membership. It's the biblical option that sees membership as a gift, something to be treasured. Membership means we have the opportunity to serve and give rather than the legalistic option to do so.

Our entire attitude is different when we approach membership the biblical way.

The Biblical Perspective of the Gift of Church Membership

I became a follower of Christ as a teenager. My high school football coach, Joe Hendrickson, showed me this verse in the Bible: "For all have sinned and fall short of the glory of God" (Rom. 3:23). He explained to me that everyone is a sinner. No one deserves salvation. Everyone deserves death (see Rom. 6:23).

But Coach Hendrickson showed me that Jesus took the punishment for me. He was my substitute on the cross. He became sin for me: "He made the One who did not know sin to be sin for us, so that we might become the righteousness of God in Him" (2 Cor. 5:21).

That evening, after my coach shared the gospel with me, I repented of my sins and placed my faith in Jesus Christ: "Therefore repent and turn back, so that your sins may be wiped out, that seasons of refreshing may come from the presence of the Lord" (Acts 3:19).

When we repent of sin and place our faith in Jesus Christ, we receive the gift of salvation: "For you are saved by grace through faith, and this is not from yourselves; it is God's gift—not from works, so that no one can boast" (Eph. 2:8–9).

Throughout the Bible, we see verse after verse that speaks of the gift of salvation, the gift of Christ's work for us, and the gift that means we cannot earn salvation through our own works.

When we receive the gift of salvation, we become part of the body of Christ. Right before the apostle Paul notes some of the gifts of the Spirit, he writes these words: "Now you are the body of Christ, and individual members of it. And God has placed these in the church" (1 Cor. 12:27–28).

Do you see what's taking place? You received a gift, the free gift of eternal salvation. That gift includes eternal salvation. It includes forgiveness of sins by Christ's death on the cross. It includes adoption by God the Father. It includes the indwelling of the Holy Spirit.

And it includes becoming a part of the body of Christ.

That's right: membership in the body of Christ, the church, is gift from God.

It's not a legalistic obligation. It's not country club perks. It's not a license for entitlements.

It's a gift. A gift from God. A gift that we should treasure with great joy and anticipation.

Universal Church or Local Church?

Now some will argue that the body of Christ refers to the universal church. The universal church means all believers everywhere for all ages.

They would be right.

But the universal church and the local church are not mutually exclusive. To the contrary, the majority of the New Testament books are written about and to local churches. The book of Acts provides a historical narrative of the Spirit's work of the churches in Jerusalem, in Antioch, in Cyprus, in Antioch in Pisidia, in Inconium, in Lystra, in Pamphylia, in Macedonia, in Thyatira, in Thessalonica, in Berea, in Athens, in Corinth, in Caesarea, in Ephesus, in Troas, in Rome, in Malta, and others.

Look at how many New Testament books were written to specific local churches: Romans, 1 Corinthians, 2 Corinthians, Galatians, Ephesians, Philippians, Colossians, 1 Thessalonians, and 2 Thessalonians. Four of Paul's books were written to individuals in specific church contexts: 1 Timothy, 2 Timothy, Titus, and Philemon. Even the book of Revelation has the context of letters to local churches.

The point? It's a lame and invalid excuse to say you will limit your involvement to the universal church. The Bible is clear that we are to be connected to a specific church in a specific context.

Understand the Gift

Church membership is a gift. A gift must be treasured. It should not be taken for granted or considered lightly. Because it is a gift, we must always be thankful for it. And when we are thankful for something, we have less time and energy to be negative.

When we receive a gift with true appreciation, we naturally want to respond to the Giver. We, therefore, see service to God as a natural outflow of the joy of our salvation and the consequent joy of our church membership. We consider it a privilege to serve the King, so we look for those opportunities at the church where we serve.

When we receive a gift, we respond with appreciation to the Giver's entire family. Other church members who have received the gift of salvation are adopted sons and daughters of God just as you are. They are not perfect, just as you aren't perfect. They are hypocrites, just as you are. But, because of your abundant joy from receiving the gift of salvation, you serve other church members with that same joy.

Healthy church membership means you find your joy in being last, instead of seeking your way and being first.

Look at this passage from Matthew 20:26–28. The context is some of Jesus' disciples seeking to be first, to get their own way. (Sound familiar?) Jesus then brings them together and tells them their attitudes stink. Okay, He didn't use that word, but He meant it.

So Jesus tells them what it means to be His true follower: "It must not be like that among you. On the contrary, whoever wants to become great among you must be your servant, and whoever wants to be first among you must be your slave; just as the Son of Man did not come to be served, but to serve, and to give His life—a ransom for many."

Get the picture? Church membership is a gift. We respond to gifts with gratitude. And one key way we express our gratitude is to serve like Jesus did and like He told us to do.

My guess is that churches would be a lot healthier if members decided to serve and to be last.

It can start with you.

The Sixth Pledge

When we have an attitude of entitlement, we have a lousy attitude. We are always looking for what we rightly deserve. And we get indignant when we don't get our way.

But when we see life, salvation, and church membership as gifts, our whole perspective changes. We don't have any sense of entitlement or expectation. To the contrary, we want to be last and receive the least because that's the way Jesus did it. And we want to be more like Him.

Church membership is a gift, a joyous gift.
Treat it as such.

The Sixth Pledge
I am a church member.

This membership is a gift. When I received the
free gift of salvation through Jesus Christ, I became
a part of the body of Christ. I soon thereafter
identified with a local body and was baptized. And
now I am humbled and honored to serve and to love
others in our church. I pray that I will never take
my membership for granted, but see it as a gift and
an opportunity to serve others and to be a part of
something so much greater than any one person or
member.

Sign and Date

Questions for Study

1. How does the gift of salvation relate to the gift of church membership?

2. Why do many church members have a sense of entitlement? What does the Bible say about that?

3. Explain how Christians are in both the universal church and in the local church.

4. Read the entire story of Jesus rebuking His disciples in Matthew 20:20–28. How could that story relate to church membership?

5. For your last question, look at each part of the entire membership covenant you have reviewed to this point. As you

look at the entire covenant, what areas will be your greatest challenge? In what areas can you make immediate changes?

ᖫ ᖫ ᖫ

I Am a Church Member

I am a church member.

I like the metaphor of membership. It's not membership as in a civic organization or a country club. It's the kind of membership given to us in 1 Corinthians 12: "Now you are the body of Christ, and individual members of it" (1 Cor. 12:27). Because I am a member of the body of Christ, I must be a functioning member, whether I am an "eye," an "ear," or a "hand." As a functioning member, I will give. I will serve. I will minister. I will evangelize. I will study. I will seek to be a blessing to others. I will remember that "if one member suffers, all the members suffer with it; if one member is honored, all the members rejoice with it" (1 Cor. 12:26).

I am a church member.

I will seek to be a source of unity in the church. I know there are no perfect pastors, staff, or other church members. But neither am I. I will not be a source of gossip or dissension. One of the greatest contributions I can make is to do all I can in God's power to help keep the church in unity for the sake of the gospel.

I am a church member.

I will not let my church be about my preferences and desires. That is self-serving. I am in this church to serve others and to serve Christ. My Savior went to a cross for me. I can deal with any inconveniences and matters that are just not my preference or style.

I am a church member.

I will pray for my pastor every day. His work is never-ending. His days are filled with constant demands for his time—with the need to prepare sermons, with those who are rejoicing in births, with those who are traveling through the valley of the shadow of death, with critics, with the hurts and hopes of others, and with the need to be a husband and a father. My pastor cannot serve our church in his own power. I will pray for God's strength for him and his family every day.

I am a church member.

I will lead my family to be good members of this church as well. We will pray together for our church. We will *worship together in our church. We will serve together in our church. And we will ask Christ to help us fall deeper in love with this church, because He gave His life for her.*

I am a church member.

This membership is a gift. When I received the free gift of salvation through Jesus Christ, I became a part of the body of Christ. I soon thereafter identified with a local body and was baptized. And now I am humbled and honored to serve and to love others in our church. I pray that I will never take my membership for granted, but see it as a gift and an opportunity to serve others and to be a part of something so much greater than any one person or member.

I am a church member.
And I thank God that I am.

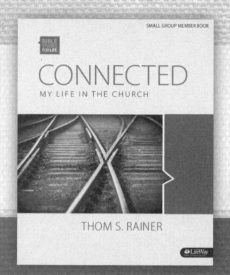

Great follow up to
I Am a Church Member

Join Thom S. Rainer for the six-session, small group study from Ephesians on the honor, privilege, and responsibility of being connected to the body of Christ—to the church.

Leader Kit includes:
- *Group Member Book** with leader helps
- DVD with short videos featuring Thom Rainer for use in each session
- Downloadable campaign materials

* Print, digital, and app formats

thomrainer.com/connected